The Proceedings of the Laymen's Convention of the M. E. Church, Genesee Conference, held at Albion, December, 1858.

First Fruits Press
Wilmore, Kentucky
c2017

The proceedings of the Laymen's Convention of the M. E. Church, Genesee Conference, held at Albion, December, 1858.

First Fruits Press, ©2017
Previously published by the Commercial Advertiser Steam Press, 1859.

ISBN: 9781621716556 (print), 9781621716563 (digital), 9781621716570 (kindle)

Digital version at http://place.asburyseminary.edu/freemethodistbooks/29/

For all other uses, contact:

First Fruits Press
B.L. Fisher Library
Asbury Theological Seminary
204 N. Lexington Ave.
Wilmore, KY 40390
http://place.asburyseminary.edu/firstfruits

Layman's Convention of the Methodist Episcopal Church, Genesee Conference (1859 : Albion, N.Y.)
   The proceedings of the Laymen's Convention of the M. E. Church, Genesee Conference, held at Albion, December, 1858.--Wilmore, Kentucky : First Fruits Press, ©2017.
      22, [4] pages; 21 cm.
      Reprint. Previously published: Buffalo, [New York] : Commercial Advertiser Steam Press, 1859.
      ISBN 9781621716556 (pbk.)
      1. Methodist Episcopal Church. Genesee Conference--Congresses. 2. Church controversies--Methodist Episcopal Church. 3. Free Methodist Church of North America--History. 4. Methodist Episcopal Church. Genesee Conference--History. I. Title. II. Methodist Episcopal Church. Genesee Conference.
BX8235.L39 1859

Cover design by Jon Ramsay

asburyseminary.edu
800.2ASBURY
204 North Lexington Avenue
Wilmore, Kentucky 40390

First Fruits
THE ACADEMIC OPEN PRESS OF ASBURY SEMINARY

First Fruits Press
The Academic Open Press of Asbury Theological Seminary
204 N. Lexington Ave., Wilmore, KY 40390
859-858-2236
first.fruits@asburyseminary.edu
asbury.to/firstfruits

THE PROCEEDINGS

OF THE

LAYMEN'S CONVENTION

OF THE

M. E. Church, Genesee Conference,

HELD AT

ALBION, DECEMBER, 1858.

———————

BUFFALO:
COMMERCIAL ADVERTISER STEAM PRESS.
1859.

PROCEEDINGS

OF THE

LAYMEN'S CONVENTION,

HELD AT

Albion, December 1 and 2, 1858.

On Wednesday, pursuant to the notice in the Call, the members of the Convention met in the M. E. Church at Albion, for the purpose of commencing the Convention with a Laymen's Love Feast. It was a season of much interest. At 8½ P. M. the Love Feast was closed, and the Convention adjourned to Kingsland Hall, for the purpose of organizing.

The Convention was organized by the election of the following officers:

President.
ABNER J. WOOD, of Parma.

Vice-Presidents.

I. M. CHESBROUGH, Pekin,   G. C. SHELDON, Allegany,
G. W. HOLMES, Kendall,   J. H. BROOKS, Olean,
S. C. SPRINGER, Gowanda,   GEO. BASCOM, Allegany,
C. SANDFORD, Perry.

Secretaries.

S. K. J. CHESBROUGH, Pekin,   W. H. DOYLE, Youngstown,
J. A. LATTA, Brockport.

Committee on Resolutions.

S. K. J. CHESBROUGH, Pekin,   S. S. RICE, Clarkson,
W. H. DOYLE, Youngstown,   JOHN BILLINGS, Wilson,
G. W. ESTES, Brockport,   A. AMES, Ridgeville,
J. HANDLY, Perry.

Committee on Finance.

NELSON COE,   C. BRAINARD,   S. P. BRIGGS,   S. S. BRYANT,   GEO. HOLMES.

The Convention was addressed by I. M. CHESBROUGH, Bro. ECKLER, Bro A. CASTLE, and S. K. J. CHESBROUGH.

On motion, adjourned to 9 o'clock Thursday morning.

Thursday Morning.

Convention met at 9 A. M., A. J. WOOD in the chair. Convention opened with prayer by ALANSON REDDY.

The following Call was then read:

GENESEE CONFERENCE LAYMEN'S CONVENTION.

There has been manifested for several years past, a disposition among certain members of the Genesee Conference, to put down, under the name of fanaticism, and other opprobrious epithets, what we consider the life and power of our holy Christianity. In pursuance of this design, by reason of a combination entered into against them by certain preachers, the Rev. Isaac C. Kingsley, and Rev. Loren Stiles, Jr., were removed from the Cabinet at the Medina Conference; and the last Conference at Perry, after a trial marked by unfairness and injustice, expelled from the Conference and the Church two of our beloved brethren, Benjamin T. Roberts, and Joseph McCreery,—for no other reason, as we conceive, than that they were active and zealous ministers of our Lord Jesus Christ, and were in favor with the people, contending earnestly for those peculiarities of Methodism which have hitherto been essential for our success as a denomination; and have also dropped from the Conference two worthy, pious and devoted young men, viz, Frank M. Warner, and Isaac Foster, who, during their Conference probation, approved themselves more than ordinarily acceptable and useful among the people; and also at the last session of the Conference removed from the Cabinet Rev. C. D. Burlingham, the only remaining Presiding Elder who opposed their sway. For several years past they have also, by consummate "clerical diplomacy," removed many of our worthy members from official relation to the Church, for no other reason than that they approved of the principles advocated by these brethren.

Therefore, in view of these facts, and others of a similar nature, we, the undersigned, hereby invite all our brethren who, with us, are opposed to this proscriptive policy, to meet with us in Convention at Albion, on Wednesday and Thursday, December 1st and 2d instant, to take such action and adopt such a course as the exigencies of the case may demand. Brethren, the time has come when we are to act with decision in this matter. The convention will commence Wednesday evening at 7 o'clock, by holding a laymen's love feast. We hope our brethren who are with us in this matter will attend.

PEKIN.—I. M. Chesbrough, R. Wilcox, J. S. Mitchell, J. B. Pike, G. P. Rose, S. K. J. Chesbrough, Geo. W. Carl, J. P. Raymond.

BROCKPORT.—I. A. Latta, Franklin Smith.

WEST CARLTON.—Jesse Murdock, Chester Williams, Alanson Reddy.

GOWANDA.—A. L. Chaffee, J. H. Chaffee, S. C. Springer, Nathan C. Cass, Titus Roberts, Wm. S. Smallwood.

NIAGARA FALLS.—I. F. Fairchild, Jr., D. B. Ingraham, John Cannon, Sr., J. H. Jones.

EAST CLARKSON.—S. S. Rice, Ashel Tyler, John Shank, James M. Cusic, John Clow, George Marsellus, M. Moore, John Moore, David Hoy, John Hoy, Henry Rice, George W. Estis, Henry Moore, Henry W. Moore, Henry Fosmore, John Windust, A. Dual, Isaac Secor, Wm. P. Rice, William H. Thompson, Daniel Sinclair.

SPENCERPORT.—I. B. Cottrell, Zenas Brice, Andrew Van Zile.

NORTH CHILI.—Thomas Hanna, John Emmons, Alexander Patten, Wm. Porter, Henry Smith, Wm. Hutchins, Claudius Brainard, John Prue.

RIDGEVILLE.—Ulysses Hecox, H. E. Gregory, M. N. Downing, A. Ames, Henry Rickard, J. R. Hunt, T. Corliss, J. Corliss.

SOMERSET.—John Putman.

ALBION.—J. R. Annis, N. Brown.

YOUNGSTOWN.—John Hutchinson, Christopher Quade, W. H. Doyle, Charles Quade, Daniel Baker, S. H. Baker, William Perry, Warren Baker, Andrew Andrews.

ALLEGANY.—George Bascom, G. C. Sheldon, W. C. Bockoven, H. Chamberlain, John D. Ellis, R. R. Eggleston, J. B. Freeland.

PERRY.—J. Stainton, T. B. Catton.

MIDDLEPORT.—Henry McClean, Isaac C. Vail, Charles Jackson, David Welch.

KENDALL.—G. W. Holmes, L. Halstead, Nelson Coe, G. W. Thomas, Amos Cowell, William Nobles, A. Wheeler.

CARYVILLE.—Darius King, John D. Steadman, Thomas Chappell, Edward Tuttle, William Galliford, Richard Galliford, Thomas Halway, M. T. Dailey, Richard Stevens, O. C. Allen, Lorenzo Torrey, John Isaac, William Manning, Richard Rice, Thomas Brierly, Ebenezer Hart.

SWEDEN.—Loren Hill, F. A. Ladue.

OLEAN.—William P. Culver, T. V. Oviatt, F. Blackman, Z. Nobles, J. H. Brooks, R. A. Brooks, A. C. Brooks.

Parma Centre.—A. B. Castle, A. J. Wood, C. A. Knox, B. Burritt, Peter Van Zile, D. A. Wellman, P. Curtis, Jr., J. Fowler, S. M. Woodruff, Fayette Wood, L. S. Bryan, George Curtis, I. Walker, Elias Curtis, P. Curtis, A. Garlock, James Ireland.

Burk Hill Charge.—Mark N. Velzy, Burton Patridge, George W. Coleman.

Gainesville.—Hiram Parish, John Sherwood, Anson Card, Rufus Chamberlain, Elisha Brainard, George W. Humphreys.

After the reading of the call, the following persons gave in their names as Laymen, who fully endorsed the sentiments expressed in the call, and who were present to act accordingly. One hundred and ninety-five responded. Their names, and the respective charges to which they belong, are as follows:

Buffalo—13th St.
Dr. J. A. Campbell.

Attica.
C. R. Reynolds.

Ridgeville.
Moses N. Downing,
Ulyssus R. Hecox,
J. R. Hunt,
Anthony Ames.

Youngstown.
William H. Doyle.

Wilson.
J. G. Robinson,
A. Dailey,
Albert Whitney,
John Billings.

Charlotte & Alcott.
S. Post,
C. Lewis,
E. Eshbaugh.

Allegany.
G. C. Sheldon.

West Falls.
L. Woods.

Lockport.
R. Abbey,
J. H. Blosser,
N. B. Shearer,
Joseph Gatchell.

Niagara Falls.
D. B. Ingraham.

Yates.
H. De Line,
S. Wood,
J. Lott,
C. Johnson,
William H. Lott.
William Parsons,
Isaac C. Parsons,
A. Lott,
J. Fuller,
W. De Line,
George Clark.

Medina.
J. G. Codd,
J. M. Hills.
J. Williams,

Akron.
M. Osborn.

Pekin.
Isaac M. Chesbrough,
R. Wilcox,
J. B. Pike,
S. K. J. Chesbrough,
George P. Rose,
James P. Raymond,
Judah S. Mitchell,
John Pletcher.

Batavia.
William Jones,
George Wilson,
George Body,
James McAlpine.

Caryville.
M. T. Dailey,
Richard Stevens,
William Manning,
Thomas Chappell,
Darius King.

Byron.
M. Andrews.

Smithport.
W. J. Colgrove.

West Carlton.
O. S. Waters.

Sweden.
Lorrin Hill,
T. S. La Due,
C. S. La Due,
S. B. Saunders,
John Cowen,
A. Robinson,
C. L. Steves.

Clarkson.
A. Deuel,
S. S. Rice,
John Hoy,
David Hoy,
Wilson Moore,
John Windust,
George W. Estes,
John Shank,
Henry Moore,

Kendall.
N. Coe,
Amos Cowell,
Stephen Jencks,
J. Higley,
N. S. Bennet,
William Noble,
Jesse Fountain,
Alfred Hornsby,
William Nichols,
G. W. Holmes,
L. F. Halstead,
A. N. Spears,
Robert Scott.

West Barre.
Squire Burns,
Edward Parker,
Hiram Snell,
R. M. Tinkham,
J. Sandford,

Millville.
J. E. Castle,
Watson Case,
B. E. Seaver,

Alabama.
J. C. Vincent.

Le Roy.
R. Teasdale.

Hulberton.
E. W. Butterfield,
M. Terry,
R. Huff,
William Knight.

Somerset.
G. G. Rice,
John Putman,
Adam Miller,
J. Nelson,
Thomas Sherrif.

North Chili.
C. Brainard,
William Porter,
T. Hanah,
A. Armin,
John Prue,
A. Patten,
Henry Smith.

Murray.
John M. Brace.

Brockport.
J. A. Latta,
T. C. Cowen,
A. Moore,
Franklin Smith,
E. L. Shepard.

Albion.
J. R. Annis,
J. Whitney,
R. C. Van Antwerp,
J. M. Brace,
E. W. Mott,
W. Van Antwerp,
Lewis Howe,
C. B. Pierson,
Albert Benton,
J. Hubbard,
M. L. Fuller,
N. F. Chapin,
William Graham,
M. H. Bronson,
S. M. Forbes,
C. Crandall,
S. P. Briggs,
M. A. Dunning,
G. W. Woodard,
Benjamin Babcock,
A. H. Paine,
Alfred Hill,
Henry Wilson,
James Graham,
C. Babcock,
D. E. Tyler,
N. H. Brown,
D. J. Braman.

Asbury.
M. Seekins,
C. Sperry,
H. S. Husted,
S. Near.

8

Parma.
A. J. Wood,
B. Burritt,
S. M. Woodruff,
P. Van Zile,
L. S. Bryan,
A. B. Castle,
Fayette Wood,
J. Fowler.

Gowanda.
Titus Roberts,
S. C. Springer,
N. C. Cass.

Barre.
J. G. Sanborn.

Perry.
T. B. Catton,
J. Handley,
David Gates,
Clark Sandford.

North Greece.
L. S. Bryan.

County Line.
John Haland.

Pavilion.
A. Pickard,
E. W. Hutchinson.

East Carlton.
Lewis Steadman.

Covington.
T. H. Jeffres,
M. W. Velzey,
James Velzey,
W. C. Bainbridge,
G. W. Pattridge.
A. H. Green,
L. B. Wolcott,
S. Heath.

West Carlton.
Jesse Murdock,
Thomas Ekel,
Alanson Reddy,
O. L. Waters.

Knowlesville.
G. W. Furgerson,
O. L. Walters,
J. O. Brown.

Olean.
J. H. Brooks,
S. J. Nobles.

Spencerport.
A. Atchison,
A. Van Zile.

Royalton & Middleport.
David Welch,
Philo Ames,
F. M. Warner.

On motion of Brother ESTES, it was moved and carried that no member of this Convention should speak more than once on any one question, until all others who wished to speak had spoken. And that no one be allowed to speak more than five minutes.

On motion of Brother ESTES, it was moved and carried that none be allowed to speak or vote in the Convention on any question, who is not in sympathy with this Convention and approves of the object set forth in the call.

The Committee on Resolutions came in and presented the following Report, which was read to the Convention:

As members of the Church of Jesus Christ, we have the deepest interest in the purity of her ministers. To them we look for instruction in those things that affect our everlasting welfare.

Their ministrations and their example influence us to a far greater extent than we are perhaps aware of. As Methodists, we have no voice in deciding who shall be our respective pastors. Any one of a hundred, whom those holding the reins of power may select, may be sent to us, and we are expected to receive and sustain him. We may then properly feel and express a solicitude for the purity of the ministry at large, and especially for that portion of it comprising the Genesee Conference, within the bounds of which we reside.

In the New Testament we learn that the Apostles, enjoying as they did the inspiration of the Holy Ghost, were accustomed, on important occasions, to consult the brethren at large, and to proceed according to their expressed decisions. We claim that reason and revelation both, give us the right to form and express our opinions of the public actions of the ministers who occupy our pulpits and are sustained by our contributions. In theory, at least, we as Protestants, deny the doctrine of infallibility. It is possible for a majority of a Conference to be mistaken; it is also possible that they may take action which is unjust and wicked. We believe that Conferences, as well as other public bodies, may err, and that their acts are proper subjects of criticism, to approve or condemn, as the case may demand; and that individual members, for an honest expression of their convictions, ought not to be rewarded with proscription or excommunication; otherwise concealment and corruption would be the order of the day.

We look upon the expulsion of brothers Roberts and McCreery as an act of wicked persecution, calling for the strongest condemnation. It was also a palpable violation of that freedom of speech and of the press, which is guaranteed to all by our free institutions.

The facts, as we understand them, are these: For years past, among the preachers, there has prevailed a division, growing out of the connection of some with secret societies—a diversity of views upon the doctrine of holiness, and the holding of different views of the standard of justification.

Writers of the Regency party published, in "The Advocate" and other papers, articles doing great injustice to those who were trying to keep up the old land-marks of Methodism. Their partisan representations were producing their designed effects. Many felt that the time had come when a representation of the other side ought to be made.

Accordingly, Rev. B. T. Roberts wrote an article under the title of "New School Methodism," setting forth his views of the questions at issue. The candor and good spirit of his article is apparent. We have ourselves heard different preachers in sympathy with the "Regency party" set forth views similar to those ascribed to them in "New School Methodism."

For writing this article, a charge of *immorality* was preferred against Rev. B. T. Roberts. He stated in open Conference to the party who accused him, that if he had misrepresented them, he would correct and publish his mistake. No correction was made; no one claimed to have been misrepresented.

The charges were sustained by a majority vote, though in the specifications he was accused of having written what no honest construction of his words would bear. It was eagerly published far and wide, that this useful preacher had been convicted of "immoral and unchristian conduct." To satisfy the general anxiety and desire to know in what the "immorality" consisted, one of our number published a second edition of "New School Methodism," the charges and specifications, and a short account of the trial. For circulating this document, these two brethren were tried at the last Conference for "immoral and unchristian conduct," and expelled. One witness, and one only, Rev. J. Bowman, testified that Brother R. handed him a package of these pamphlets for circulation, but which he never circulated.

Had the specifications been proved ever so clearly, they would not have constituted an offence *deserving of censure.* Upon such grounds were these men of God, Brothers Roberts and McCreery, expelled from the Conference and the Church. It would have been reasonable to have supposed that common malignity would have been satisfied with deposing them from the ministry. But such was the malevolence of those controlling a majority of the votes of Conference, that they could not stop short of the utmost limit of their power. Had they not been restrained by the civil law, the fires of martyrdom might have been kindled in the nineteenth century in western New York.

So trifling was the accusation against these brethren, that in all the efforts that have been made to vindicate those voting for their condemnation, no one has attempted to show that the testimony justified the decision. Their only defence is, "If these men did not deserve to be expelled for circulating the pamphlet, they did for promoting enthusiasm and fanaticism." If so, why were they not tried for it? Where is the justice of trying men for one thing, and condemning them for another?

In reference to this charge of "fanaticism and enthusiasm," we feel prepared to speak. Our means of information are far more reliable than that of those preachers who bring the accusation. We have attended the "camp meetings and General Quarterly meetings," against which a special outcry has been made as the "hot-beds of enthusiasm." We have sat under the preaching of these brethren who are charged with promoting these disorders—have heard some of them by the year. *We know what Methodism is;* some of us were converted, and joined the church under the labors of her honored pioneers. We speak advisedly then, when we say that the charge brought against brothers Roberts and McCreery, and the class of preachers denominated "Nazarites," of promoting fanaticism, is *utterly false and groundless.* They are simply trying to have us in earnest to gain heaven. Instead of attacking the church, they are its defenders. They preach the doctrines of the Methodist church, as we used to hear them preached years ago; and through their instrumentality many have been made to rejoice in the enjoyment of a PRESENT AND FULL SALVATION. We cannot say this of their opposers. The Regency affirm that they preach the doctrines of holiness. We have yet to learn of the first person who has of late years experienced this blessing through their instrumentality. On the contrary, we believe some of them have put down the standard of justification far below what Methodism and the Scriptures will warrant. Whether, therefore, we consider the ostensible, or the real cause of the expulsion of Bros. Roberts and McCreery, the act calls for and receives our hearty and earnest condemnation.

Nor can we pass by, as undeserving of notice, the course pursued by the "Regency party," whenever complaints of a serious character have been brought against any of their number.

Reports that some of them have been guilty of "crimes expressly forbidden in the word of God," and involving a high degree of moral turpitude, have been current. Complaints have been made, and though the proof of their guilt was deemed ample, yet they have been summarily dismissed, and in such a way as to discourage all efforts to bring to justice before the Conference, any of the "Regency" preachers, no matter how wicked and immoral he may be.

Whether in their secret meetings, (the existence of which they at first so stoutly denied, but afterwards attempted to defend, when they were fully exposed,) any combination, expressed or implied, was entered into to screen their guilty partisans, and persecute their innocent opposers, we have no means of knowing, but it appears to us that such has been the result. That we can have confidence in the Christian character of those whose votes are given to condemn the innocent, and to screen the guilty, is impossible. We also strongly disapprove and condemn the course taken by the dominant party in keeping out of Conference young men of approved piety, talent, and promise, simply because they have too much Christian manliness and conscience to become the tools of designing and ambitious men. We are true, loyal, God-fearing Methodists. We have not the slightest intention of leaving the church of our choice. We believe the evils complained of may be cured, and for this purpose we will leave no proper means untried.

One patent remedy is within our reach—the power to withhold our supplies. We are satisfied that no matter how strongly we may condemn the course of the Regency faction, they will not amend, so long as they are sustained. Besides, we cannot in conscience give our money to put down the work of the Lord. Therefore, we wish it distinctly understood, that we cannot pay one farthing to preacher or presiding elder, who voted for the expulsion of Bros. Roberts and McCreery, only upon "contrition, confession, and satisfactory reformation."

It may be thought by some that such action on our part is revolutionary. But from the following extracts, it will appear that we are only exercising our undisputed rights in a constitutional way.

We are giving unquestionable proofs of our loyalty to the Church, by thus endeavoring to correct one of the most oppressive and tyrannical abuses of power that was ever heard of.

We trust that none will think of leaving the Church; but let us all stand by and apply the proper legitimate remedy for the shameless outrages that have been perpetrated under the forms of justice.

We quote from an Essay on Church Polity, by Rev. Abel Stevens, LL.D. This book has been adopted by the General Conference as a text-book in the course of study for young preachers. Hence it is of the highest authority.

Dr. Stevens says, " Church Polity," page 162: " What check have the *people* on this machinery ? It is clear that as the preachers appoint the bishops, and the bishops distribute the preachers, the people should check the whole plan by a counterbalance upon the whole ministerial body. This is provided in the most decisive form that it could possibly assume, namely, the power of pecuniary supplies. No *stipulated contract* for support exists in the Methodist economy. The discipline *allows* a certain support, but does not enforce it; and no Methodist preacher *can prosecute* a civil suit for his salary. The General Conference disclaims all right to tax the property of our members.

" A Methodist Church has no necessity, in order to control or remove the preacher, to prosecute him by a tedious and expensive process at law, but simply to signify that after a given date HIS SUPPLIES CEASE. He cannot live on air; he must submit or depart.

" This would be a sufficient guaranty, certainly; and this check applies not merely to a specific prerogative of the ministry, but to the *whole* ministerial system. The lamented Dr. Emory thus states it:

" ' We have said that the Methodist Episcopal Church possesses effective and substantial security against any encroachments of tyranny on the part of her pastors. For the sober truth is, that there is not a body of ministry in the world more perfectly dependent on those whom they serve than the Methodist itinerant ministry. Our system places us, in fact, not only from year to year, or from quarter to quarter, but from week to week within the reach of such a controlling check, on the part of the people, as is possessed we verily believe, by no other denomination whatever.' "

Dr. BOND, in his " Economy of Methodism, page 35, says: " The General Conference have never considered themselves authorized to levy taxes upon the laity, or to make any pecuniary contribution a condition of membership in the Church. Our preachers are totally dependent upon the voluntary contributions of the laity; and we thereby have over them a positive and absolute control; for whenever their flocks shall withdraw their support, the preachers will be un ler the necessity of abandoning their present pastoral relation, and of betaking themselves to some secular occupation. The traveling preacher who depends for bread, both for himself and family, upon the good-will of the lay brethren, can have no temptation to any unwarrantable or odious exercise of authority over them."

In " Ecclesiastical Polity, by Rev. A. N. Fillmore," page 166, we have the following: " Methodist preachers have no means of enforcing the payment of a cent for their support, for although the Discipline provides for a certain allowance, it furnishes no means to obtain it; and there is no article even to *expose a member to censure* for neglecting or refusing to contribute for the support of the Gospel."

Thus the right to withhold supplies, upon good and sufficient reasons, is conceded and urged by standard authors of our Church. That such a reason now exists, must be apparent to every one that is not entirely blinded to the claims of justice and humanity. Nor can we approve of the action of the Bishop in appointing to the office of Presiding Elders, men who participated in the proscriptive measures of the Regency party.

We think that station ought to be filled with men who are in sympathy with the life and power of Godliness, and who are laboring to promote it. We look upon the Church as an organization established to aid in securing the salvation of souls, and not mainly to raise money.

This Convention originated among ourselves. The first suggestion was made by one of our number. Neither the brethren expelled, nor any of the members of the Conference had anything to do whatever with calling this Convention. We mention this fact, because the insinuation is frequently made, that the people can do nothing except at the instigation of the preachers. We are not papists, requiring to be instructed by the priesthood at every turn, what action we shall take, or what papers and books we shall read.

We assure our ministerial brethren, both those who have been thrust out of the Conference, and those who remain, who are devoted to the work of spreading scriptural holiness, that they have our ardent sympathy; and as long as they employ their time and talents in endeavoring to promote the life and power of Godliness, we pledge ourselves to cordially sustain them, by our influence and our means, whether they are in the Conference or not. Therefore,—

Resolved, That we have the utmost confidence in Bros. B. T. Roberts and Joseph McCreery, notwithstanding their expulsion from the Conference—

ranking them as we do among the most pure and able ministers of the New Testament.

Resolved, That we adhere to the doctrines and usages of the fathers of Methodism. Our attachment to the M. E. Church is earnest and hearty, but we do not acknowledge the oppressive policy of the secret fraternity in the Conference, known as the Buffalo Regency, as the action of the Church; and we cannot and will not submit to the same. We hold it as a gross mal-administration under the assumed sanction of judicial forms.

Resolved, That the laity are of some use to the Church, and that their views and opinions ought to command some little respect rather than that cool contempt with which their wishes have been treated by some of the officials of the Conference, for several years past.

Resolved, That the farcical cry of disunion and secession is the artful production of designing men, to frighten the feeble and timid into their plans of operation and proscription. We wish to have it distinctly understood that we have not, and never had, the slightest intention of leaving the church of our choice, and that we heartily approve of the course of Bros. Roberts and McCreery in re-joining the church at their first opportunity; and we hope that the oppressive and un-methodistic administration indicated in the pastoral address as the current policy of the majority of the Conference, will not drive any of our brethren from the church. Methodists have a better right in the Methodist Episcopal Church than anybody else, and by *God's* grace in it we intend to remain.

Resolved, That it is a matter of no small grievance and of detriment to the church of *God* that these preachers, in their local, pastoral administration, have deliberately set themselves to exclude from official position in the church, leaders, stewards, and trustees, members of deep and undoubted Christian experience, because of their adhesion to spiritual religious Methodism, and to supply their places with persons of slight and superficial religious experience, because of their adhesion to a worldly policy Methodism.

Resolved, That we will not aid in the support of any member of the Genesee Conference who assisted, either by his vote or his influence, in the expulsion of Bros. Roberts and McCreery from the Conference and the Church, until they are fully reinstated to their former position; and that we do recommend all those who believe that these brethren have been *unjustly* expelled from the Conference and the Church, to take the same course.

Resolved, That we recommend Rev. B. T. Roberts and Rev. J. McCreery to travel at large, and labor as opportunity presents, for the promoting of the work of God and the salvation of souls.

Resolved, That we recommend that Bro. Roberts locate his family in the city of Buffalo.

Resolved, That in our opinion Bro. Roberts should receive $1,000 for his support during the ensuing year, and Bro. McCreery should receive $600.

Resolved, That we recommend the appointment of a committee of fifteen to carry out the above resolutions, each of whom shall be authorized to appoint collectors as they may deem necessary; and we also recommend the appointment of a treasurer, to whom all moneys received for the purpose shall be paid, and who shall pay out the same, pro rata, to Bros. Roberts and McCreery, and receive their receipts for the same.

Resolved, That a copy of the foregoing preamble and resolutions be forwarded to the *Northern Independent,* with a request that the same be published.

S. K. J. CHESBROUGH, Pekin,
WILLIAM H. DOYLE, Youngstown,
GEORGE W. ESTES, Brockport,
S. S. RICE, Clarkson,
JOHN BILLINGS, Wilson,
JONATHAN HANDLEY, Perry,
ANTHONY AMES, Ridgeville,
Committee on Resolutions.

The first Resolution was read the second time, and passed by a unanimous vote.
The second Resolution was read, and passed, by a unanimous vote.
The third Resolution was read, and passed, by a unanimous vote.
The fourth Resolution was read.

Br. JEFFERS, of Covington, was not willing that the Committee on Resolutions should do all the thinking and speaking for us. I came here for light; I came here to be instructed.

After several brethren had spoken upon the propriety of using the words " designing men," the Resolution was passed by a unanimous vote.

The fifth Resolution was then read, and called forth a spirited discussion, in which several of the brethren engaged.

Bro. T. H. JEFFERS, of Covington, said: Mr. President—the Committee state certain things in respect to appointments, removals, and nominations to church offices, which I, for one, do not, from personal knowledge, know to be true; I may believe them, but I wish to know. I am down here from old Covington circuit, in charge of which the conference has not yet ventured to put one of the preachers of that faction whose policy is censured in this resolution. The expense of enslaving us to this policy, will cost more than the experiment is worth, I mistrust, when it shall be tried. But I do not wish to vote what I do not know personally. When called in question for my vote, I want an answer ready. I call for the testimony under this specification.

Bro. DUNHAM, of Knowlesville, though usually in favor of expedition in public meetings, was nevertheless, glad to see a debate opened on this resolution. Does this resolution call in question the right of the preacher to remove and appoint leaders, and to nominate and thereby virtually appoint stewards and trustees as prescribed in the discipline? He hoped we should be guarded, and give no just occasion to be charged with disloyalty and revolutionary insubordination. He wanted all grievances redressed in an orderly and constitutional way, if possible.

Bro. G. W. ESTES, of Clarkson, said: Not at all. It is everywhere conceded that the preacher has a perfect disciplinary right to appoint whomsoever he pleases to the leadership, and to nominate whom he pleases for stewards and trustees. Would to God, they would observe the discipline as closely in some other matters also. We have no controversy with the law, or its legitimate administration. The law is good, when methodistically administered; but when a foreign, unmethodistic power steps in to administer it, contrary to its obvious import and spirit, such administration becomes a grievance, and a detriment to the church. It is virtually, if not literally, a maladministration, and should be corrected. If the preacher wishes to appoint an idiot or a blackleg leader, or nominate him steward or trustee, no one will question his prerogative to do so; it is his right under the law. But we have a right to feel aggrieved at it, and to say so. And that is all that this resolution does. What is complained of in this resolution has been done all through this land. The "orders in council" to this effect were published in the Buffalo organ of the faction more than three years ago, and have been faithfully executed whenever practicable to do so. At Brockport, a man (here present) was trustee year after year, while a backslider, and out of the church. But as soon as he got religion, and began to pray in his family, and joined the church, and attended class and prayer meetings, he was turned out of the trusteeship at the very next election, through the intrigues of the preacher. His religion was such as spoilt him for the office. It was of the sort to make a difference in him from what he was before, and thus disqualified him for official position in the church. Salvation is at a heavy discount in Brockport. But there is a little in bank there yet, glory to God!

Bro. J. SMITH, of Brockport: Yes, that is so; bless the Lord! After all our persecutions, there are some left in Brockport who have survived the removal of leaders; and what is more, the appointment of leaders. Bro. Estes has spoken somewhat of our affairs, and in so doing, has called me out. But the half has not been told. Bro. Estes was once leader there; I was also. His class and mine were well filled always—his to over-flowing. Everybody, as fast as they got religion, wanted to join one or the other of these classes. The "fanaticism," as it was called, predominated in them, and drew a room full every time. If the preacher came in to try and stem the tide, it was of no use; it swept over him like a rush. Soon the classes were divided, and cut up in a way to stop the "fanaticism," as God's work was called. Some of the live ones were put into another class under a secret society leader, to cool them down. But when he came to meet his class, there were present, all told, one traveling preacher, one local preacher, one leader, and one poor pious colored girl, who thought she must meet class where she was set to. She protested against being thought of so much consequence as to require two preachers and one leader to lead her; so she fled back to the fold again. Soon our class-books were called for to be looked over, and were kept for nine weeks, during which time nobody knew who was leader. After a while, Bro. Estes was removed, and at length, I also. There seemed to be a harder effort to kill out the life and power of religion, than to get souls saved; and all the appointments by the preacher seemed to look in that direction. The resolution is emphatically appropriate, as far as the administration in Brockport is concerned.

Bro. J. B. CATTON said: I hail from Perry. We had a session of the Genesee Conference there lately; therefore we are here. We had a leader of twenty years standing; he had stood through thick and thin; he was not a man to be spoken against. Like leader, like class. There was life and power in our class and prayer meetings; just as there had been from the beginning. We were chiefly English, and knew what Methodism was. Two years ago, (I call no names—the minutes will show who was our preacher,) the preacher took a fancy that the sort of religion we had was a little too antiquated, or vociferous, or something of that sort; and so our class was disbanded, leader and all, and set off to other classes. This was considered an underhanded way of doing what the preacher did not dare to

2

do directly. This is not the only instance in which the heritage of the Lord has been wasted there. Perry was once a strong society—eminently Methodistic. We have slept while the enemy has been sowing tares. We have had too much confidence in our ministers. We took it for granted they were servants of God and the church, while in fact they were the servants of a secret inquisition in our midst. The conference session at Perry has opened the eyes of our people there. We presume no member of the majority will care to be stationed at Perry another year. We were chiefly English, and they counted on our methodistic loyalty to sustain the preacher they have sent us. Some will do it—if they choose.

Brother W. PARSONS of Yates, said: I hail from a quarter of the Lord's plantation where the policy complained of has been pursued as far as circumstances would admit, without provoking open insurrection. Indeed we are very little short of that condition now. At our last election for trustees, two old and substantial members were left out of the board, and their places filled by younger men, notorious for adhering to worldly-policy Methodism. Three old trustees were called upon privately, and inquired of if they would use their official influence against the Nazarites, as the religious part of the society was called. They answered that they should go in for the life and power of religion as they always had done. They were then told that they could not be elected; and all the outsiders who had ever attended meeting or who had paid a quarter at a donation, were rallied out to vote against them. The influence and management of the preacher controlled the election, as is generally the case. Since then, and no longer ago than last week, the church was locked against the funeral of one of the most aged and wealthy members, because he had selected Brother Roberts to officiate on the occasion; and this act received the public commendation of the venerable author of the Pastoral Address. There is no time to mention all the cases sustaining the grievances set forth in this resolution. But in the midst of all, they cannot hinder us from enjoying salvation in our souls; the consolations of God abound to us in the midst of all our persecutions. Glory to Jesus! a goodly number in Yates remain, who mean to be free and enjoy religion at all hazards. What the Pastoral Address means by our "exciting insubordination and enjoying religion," is this: most of those who profess to enjoy religion in Yates, refuse to pay our money for doing the work that was done at the two last Conferences; but apply it to help those brethren who are persecuted by this secret society faction in the Conference. This insubordinate conduct we propose to continue, as necessarily antecedent to enjoying religion.

Brother Jones, of Batavia, said: This resolution will be perfectly intelligible in Batavia; it will not need any comment; we have a preacher who goes the whole Regency figure with a strong hand. We had a leader there who had filled the office for many years; he was an old line Methodist; it would not sound well to remove him outright; besides this, he had a *pocket* which might have been affected adversely by open proscription; so an assistant leader, a tool of the preacher, was appointed; and being sustained by the preacher and governed by his instructions, he acted in such an outrageous manner, that our old leader, (who was a peaceful man,) gave up his class-book to avoid controversy and collision in the class-room. By this crafty means the preacher got rid of him without directly turning him out. He was a man of deep piety, and of substantial social position in the community. Also, a brother was turned out for saying "amen" in meeting. The charge against him, in imitation of Conference prosecutions, was for "unchristian and immoral conduct;" but everybody in our vicinity knew this to be only a judicial sham. About the time of the Careyville general quarterly meeting he had committed the crime of getting unreasonably blessed in meeting, even beyond an "innate sense of propriety," and was turned out of the synagogue for that "unchristian and immoral conduct." About the same time, our preacher prepared a document forbidding the saying "amen" in meeting, or anything of that sort, and wanted the official board to sign it. Our leader and some others would not do it, which made him more furious than ever. We have had great times in Batavia, but the work of God grows more and more in the midst of all these persecutions. The devil is evidently alarmed for his kingdom there, and the preacher manifests a similar concern. All these removals and appointments are only the necessary evolutions to embody his forces into a more effective array against living spiritual Methodism. But,

> We'll drive the battle on,
> We'll drive the battle on;
> In Jesus' might we'll stand the fight,
> And drive the battle on.

Brother Jeffers, of Covington, said: Now we have got the testimony in this case I think we may as well pass the resolution. All I wanted was to get the facts before this body; our living membership ought not to be imposed upon by having such officials set over them. Methodism was designed to be *officiated* by religious men; not by the menials of an inquisition, nor the ungodly devotees of worldly policy. The people ought not only to speak out but to act out—strike this Upas at the root.

On motion, the Convention adjourned, to meet again at half past one o'clock.

Afternoon Session.

Convention met.   A. L. Woon in the chair.   Prayer by Bro. ——.

The Committee on Finance reported, that we should need about twenty-five dollars to defray expenses.   On motion, a collection was then taken up, amounting to twenty-four dollars, which was decided sufficient, and the committee was discharged.

The sixth resolution was then read.

Brother JEFFRES arose and said: Mr. Chairman, we have a right, under proper circumstances, to use scripture phrases. "By the life of Pharoah" I perceive that ye are designing men! I perceive that ye are come here to act with decision. I have always been a Methodist. My mother and father were converted under the labors of John Wesley. No wonder, then, that I am so fully attached to the church of my choice. My father died before my remembrance. My mother was poor. She had to use the most rigid economy, in order to support the family; yet, amid all our penury, my mother always paid her quarterage; and I well remember how she used to say to us, " Children, quarterly meeting is coming around; we must pay our preacher; we have no money. What is to be done? You must go without butter." Yes, sir; we used to eat our bread dry, for two or three weeks; and my mother would take the butter so saved to the store, and get money to pay our preacher. This is the way my mother taught me. I may well say that I drew from my mother's breast the practice of paying the Methodist preachers. I have always done so. But, sir, in this resolution we say, that we will withhold our money from certain preachers. Sir, is there no other way to meet this difficulty? Can there be no other means used? I would to God that there could; but, sir, I can not see how we are to meet the case in any other way. It is a very strong measure, but sir, upon mature reflection, I must vote for the resolution.

Cries from all over the Convention—"Question," "question."
The resolution was then passed by a unanimous vote.

The seventh, eighth, ninth, and tenth resolutions were then unanimously passed.

The following committee were then appointed, as called for in the tenth resolution:

Isaac M. Chesbrough, *Treasurer*, Post Office address, South Pekin, Niagara Co.

Buffalo District.—A. W. Perry, Ira P. Wheeler, M. Osborn.

Niagara District.—W. H. Doyle, Isaac C. Parsons, S. K. J. Chesbrough.

Genesee District.—A. Van Zile, S. S. Rice, John Dorman.

Wyoming District.—J. Grisewood, C. Reynolds, E. J. Jeffers.

Olean District.—S. J. Noble, G. C. Sheldon, George Bascom.

The eleventh resolution was then read. A motion was made to amend by adding, "The Northern Christian Advocate.

Bro. S. K. J. Chesbrough said: Mr. Chairman, I shall oppose the amendment from personal feelings. I prepared a copy of the call for the "Northern," and mailed it myself, at the same time I mailed the one to the "Independent," but it was not published. We have every evidence, sir, that that paper is not in sympathy with us or our Convention. I am willing to write as many copies as you may order, but I think the time had better be spent in prayer, than writing for the "Northern" what we know will not be published in that paper. I thank God we have a paper through whose columns we may speak. I hope we will, to a man, sustain the "Independent."

Bro. Jeffers said: Mr. Chairman, I know what the brother has said is true; but, sir, we read of the widow and unjust judge, and though he feared neither God or man, yet lest she should weary him with her continual coming, he granted her her desire. I hope we will try again. I hope the amendment will pass.

Motion to amend lost. The resolution as read was then passed, and the preamble and resolution as a whole were adopted.

Rev. B. I. Ives, of Auburn, was called for, and came forward and addressed the Convention. His speech was such as Bro. Ives, and he only, could make. The history of the "rise and progress" of the Independent was given in such a manner as to open the eyes of many of the Convention to the importance of more fully sustaining the paper. After the conclusion of his address, the following resolution was passed:

Resolved, That the thanks of this Convention is due, and are hereby tendered to Bro. Ives for the remarks which we have had the pleasure of listening to.

It was then

Resolved, That the thanks of this Convention are hereby tendered to the inhabitants of Albion, for their kindness in entertaining the members of this Convention during their stay in the village.

Resolved, That when we adjourn, we adjourn to meet at North Bergen, June 25th, 1859; appropriate notice to be given by the President and Secretary.

The following resolutions were then passed:

Resolved, That a committee be appointed to correspond with brethren in different parts of the work upon the propriety of establishing in the city of Buffalo a periodical devoted to the advocacy of "Earnest Christianity."
The chair appointed the following committee: Rev. B. T. ROBERTS, Rev. LORIN STILES, Rev. C. D. BURLINGHAM, LEONARD HALSTEAD, S. C· SPRINGER, G. C. SHELDON.

Resolved, That we tender to the Publishing Association of the "Northern Independent," our hearty thanks for their liberality in opening their columns for the publication of our notices, and for its fearless defence of truth pertaining to our interests.

On motion, it was

Resolved, That we now commence a subscription for the support of Bros. Roberts and McCredy, as provided in the ninth resolution.

Subscriptions to $425 were made, of which $97.50 was paid in.

Convention then adjourned.

PROCEEDINGS OF THE LAYMEN'S CONVENTION

OF THE GENESEE CONFERENCE, OF THE M. E. CHURCH.

Held at Albion, November 1st and 2d, 1859. [Second Annual Session.]

BY S. K. J. CHESBROUGH, SECRETARY OF THE CONVENTION.

" Persecuted, but not forsaken;—Cast down but not destroyed."—PAUL.

On Tuesday, Nov. 1st., pursuant to the notice in the call, the members of the Convention met in the Baptist church at Albion, for the purpose of commencing the Convention with a Laymen's Love Feast.

At 9 o'clock P. M., the Love Feast was closed, when the convention proceeded to organize for business by the appointment of the following officers *pro tem:*

President, S. C. SPRINGER.
Secretaries, S. K. J. CHESBROUGH, T. SULLY.

On motion of Geo. W. Estes, a committee of fifteen on Resolutions was appointed viz:

Niagara District.
WM. H. DOYLE,
S. K. J. CHESBROUGH,
RUSSEL WILCOX.

Genesee District.
GEO. W. ESTES,
S. S. RICE,
S. P. BRIGGS.

Wyoming District.
GEO. W. COLEMAN,
THOS. B. CATTON,
WM. HART.

Buffalo District.
CHARLES DENNY,
THOMAS SULLY,
HENRY HARTSHORN.

Olean District.
S. C. SPRINGER, TITUS ROBERTS,
WM. RUMBLE.

On motion of Thomas B. Catton a committee of seven was appointed to report nominations for permanent officers of the convention, viz:

E. P. COX, ALANSON REDDY, SQUIRE BURNS, M. SEEKINS, J. HANDLEY, F. SMITH, SETH M. WOODRUFF.

Convention opened on Wednesday morning with prayer by I. M. Chesbrough, when the roll was called, and the members of the convention responded to their names.

Report of the committee to nominate permanent officers of the convention.

For President, ABNER I. WOOD.
For Vice Presidents,
Genesee District, GEO. W. HOLMES.
Niagara " JOHN BILLINGS.
Wyoming " JONATHAN HANDLEY.
Buffalo " EDWARD P. COX.
Olean " S. C. SPRINGER.

Corresponding Secretary, S. K. J. CHESBROUGH.

Assistant Secretaries, STEPHEN S. RICE.
WM. HART,
THOMAS SULLY.

Standing Committee of Supplies:—
Genesee District, J. R. ANNIS,
GEO. W. ESTES,
JOHN PRUE.

Niagara District, I. M. CHESBROUGH,
WM. H. DOYLE,
A. AMES.

Wyoming District, THOS. B. CATTON,
J. CHESTER,
W. HOLMES.

Buffalo District, THOS. SULLY,
HENRY HARTSHORN,
CLARK REYNOLDS.

Olean District, S. C. SPRINGER,
G. C. SHELDON,
JOHN HUFF.

PREAMBLE AND RESOLUTIONS.

When we met last year in Convention, we trusted that the preachers, whose course was the cause of our assembling, would be led to repentance and reformation. But our hopes have been blasted. The scripture is still true, which saith, that " evil men and seducers shall wax worse and worse, deceiving and being deceived."

That we have the right to take into consideration the public acts of a public body to which we are intimately related, cannot be denied. That such consideration has become our duty we are well satisfied. Our Lord has given us the test, " By their fruits ye shall know them." What has been the fruits for the past year of the party in conference known as the " Buffalo Regency?" Have they been such as we should expect from men of God? We are pained to be obliged to bear testimony to the fact that some occupying the place of Methodist ministers have used their influence, and bent their energies to put down under the name of " fanaticism" what we feel confident is the work of the Holy Spirit.

The course pursued by some of our preachers, in expelling from the church, members in good standing, and high repute for their christian character, because they attended our Convention in Dec. last, we look upon as cruel and oppressive, and calls for our most decided disapproval. What does the right of private judgment amount to, if we cannot exercise it without bringing down upon our heads these ecclesiastical anathemas? To our brethren who have been so used, we extend our cordial sympathy, and we assure them that our confidence in them has not diminished on account of their names being cast out as evil for the Son of man's sake. The action of the majority, in expelling from the conference and the church, four able and devoted ministers, and locating two others, upon the most frivolous pretexts, and so at variance with the principles of justice and our holy christianity, is to cause minor offences to be aggravated, when they would otherwise be overlooked. The charge against each was the convenient one of "contumacy." The specifications were in substance, the recieving as ministers those who were expelled at the previous session of the conference, and for preaching in the bounds of other men's charges. Where in the bible, or in the discipline is "contumacy" spoken of as a crime? It is a charge generally resorted to for the purpose of oppression. Let whatever the dominant power in the church may be pleased to call "contumacy" be treated as a crime, religious liberty is at an end. There is not an honest man in the conference but may be expelled for "contumacy" whenever by any means a majority can be obtained against him. There is not a member of the M. E. Church, who acts from his own convictions of right, but may be excommunicated for "contumacy" whenever his preacher is disposed to do so. Let some mandate be issued that cannot in conscience be obeyed and the guilt of contumacy is incurred. The Regency party not only expelled devoted servants of God for contumacy, but did it under the most aggravated circumstances. An annual conference possesses no power to make laws. A resolution with a penalty affixed for its violation, is to all intents and purposes a law. The Regency passed resolutions at the last session of the conference, and then tried and expelled men for violating them months before they had an existence! That any honest man can entertain any respect for such judicial action is utterly impossible. The specifications were in keeping with the charge. The first was for recognizing as ministers the expelled members of the conference. The charge was not for recognizing them as Methodist ministers; for the expelled brethren did not claim to have authority from the church. They acted simply by virtue of their commission from God. If a man believes he is called of God to preach, and God owns and blesses his labors, has he not the right thus to warn sinners to flee the wrath to come? At the second conference held by Wesley, it was asked,—Is not the will of our governors a law? The answer was emphatic—no—not by any governors, temporal or spiritual. Therefore if any Bishop wills that I should not preach the gospel, his will is no law to me. But what if he produced a law against your preaching? I am to obey God rather than man. This is the language of the founders of Methodism. How it rebukes the arrogant, popish assumptions of some of the pretended followers of Wesley.

The second specification was for preaching in other men's charges without their consent. Where is there any thing wrong in this?— What precept of the bible, what rule of the discipline is violated? Does it not evidence the faithful minister of Jesus, burning with love for souls, rather than the criminal deserving the highest censure of the church? Methodist ministers are bound by their obligations to go to the charges to which they are appointed by the conference; *but they do not promise that they will not preach any where else.* On the contrary the commission from Christ reads "Go ye into all the world and preach the gospel to every creature." The discipline says, "You have nothing to do but to save souls; therefore spend and be spent in this work; *and go always not only to those who want you, but to those who want you most. Observe, it is not your business only to preach so many times, and to take care of this or that society; but to save as many as you can; to bring as many sinners as you can to repentance, and with all your power to build them up in that holiness without which they cannot see the Lord.*" On this ground were these men of God as we esteem them, Revs. Loren Stiles Jr., John A. Wells, Wm. Cooley, and Charles D. Burlingham excommunicated by the Regency party of the Genesee Conference at its last session. Fidelity to God will not allow us to quietly acquiesce in such decisions. It is urged that we must respect the action of the church. But what is the church? Our 13th article of religion says: "The visible church of God is a congregation of faithful men, in which the pure word of God is preached, and the sacraments duly administered." *The ministers then are not " the church."* If ministers wish to have their acts respected, they must, like other men, perform *respectable* actions.

These repeated acts of expulsions, wrong as they are in themselves, deserve the stronger condemnation from the fact, scarcely attempted to be disguised, that THE OBJECT *is to prevent the work of holiness from spreading among us—to put down the life and power of Godliness in our churches, and to inaugurate in its stead the peaceable reign of a cold and heartless formalism;—*in short, to do away with what has always been a distinctive feature of Methodism. If the work which the men who were expelled both this year and last, have labored and not without success to promote, be "fanaticism," then has Methodism from the beginning been "fanaticism." Our attachment to Methodism was never stronger than it is at present, and our sympathy and our means shall be given to the men who toil and suffer to promote it. We cannot abandon at the bidding of a majority, the doctrines of Methodism and the men who defend them.

The course of the Regency in shielding members of their faction, create the suspicion that a stronger motive than any referred to lies at the foundation of their remarkable action,— *the principle of self-preservation.* It may be that the guilty, to prevent exposure, deem it necessary to expel the innocent. Their refusal to entertain charges, and their prompt acquital of one of their leaders, though clearly proved guilty of a crime sufficient to exclude him from heaven, look strongly in that direction. The recent public exposure in another conference of one of the founders of the Regency party, who took a transfer to escape from well founded suspicion, shows how a minister may pursue, unconvicted, a career of guilt for years, when "*shielded*" by secret society influences, and willing to be the servile tool of the majority.— For the evils complained of we see no other remedy within our reach, than the one we adopted last year:—WITHOLD SUPPLIES. To show that such a remedy is "constitutional" and "loyal" we have only to refer to the "proceedings" of the convention of last year and to the authorities therein quoted.

Resolved 1—That we have the utmost confidence in Revs. B. T. Roberts, J. McCreery Jr., Loren Stiles Jr., John A. Wells, Wm. Cooley, and C. D. Burlingham; believing them to be devoted servants of *God*, suffering persecution for righteousness' sake. We hereby commend them to the confidence and sympathy of the children of God wherever they may go.

Resolved 2—That we adhere to the doctrines and usages of the Fathers of Methodism, but we do not acknowledge the oppressive policy of the secret fraternity of the conference known as the Buffalo Regency, AS THE ACTION OF THE CHURCH; and we can not and will not submit to the same. We hold it as a gross maladministration under the assumed sanction of judicial forms.

Resolved 3—That we recommend Bros. B. T. Roberts, J. McCreery Jr., Loren Stiles Jr., John A. Wells, Wm. Cooley, C. D. Burlingham, John W. Reddy, and H. H. Farnsworth, to continue to labor for the promotion of the work of God and the salvation of souls, by preaching, exhorting, visiting, and praying as they have opportunity; and we hereby assure them that while they shall thus devote themselves to the work of the ministry, we will cheerfully use our means and influence for their support.

Resolved 4—That a committee be appointed to district the work, and that committee consist of five preachers and five layman;—to wit:—Revs. B. T. Roberts, J. McCreery J., Loren Stiles Jr., J. A. Wells; Wm. Cooley.— Layman—J. R. Annis, T. B. Catton, W. H. Doyle, Thos. Sully, and John Huff.

Resolved 5—That in order to keep our people who are being oppressed by the misrule of the dominant faction in the Genesee Conference from being scattered; and finally lost to our church, we recommend our brethren in the ministry to gather our people into Bands, and to encourage them to union of action and effort in the work of the Lord:

Resolved 6—That in each Band and at each preaching appointment, regular and systematic efforts be made by way of band collections and subscriptions, to secure an adequate support for our brethren in the ministry.

Resolved 7—That we will not aid in the support of any member of the Genesee Conference, who assisted, either by his vote or his influence, in the expulsion of either Bros. Roberts, McCreery, Stiles, Wells, Cooley, and Burlingham from the conference and the church, except upon "contrition, confession and satisfactory reformation," and that we do recommend all those who believe these brethren have been *unjustly* expelled from the conference and the church, to take the same course.

Resolved 8—That we repudiate and condemn the policy of some preachers, in preaching love and charity sermons in certain places, for certain purposes, and then acting in secret meetings and open conference diametrically opposite to their own teachings. "Thou therefore which teachest another teachest thou not thyself? thou that preachest a man should not steal, dost thou steal?"

Resolved 9—That we regard the intent of the five test resolution, of the late conference at Brockport, to be Anti-Methodistic, and Popish, the merest ecclesiastical tyranny. And we recommend that the preachers remaining in the conference, who have the work of God at heart, repudiate in theory and practice the aforesaid resolutions.

Resolved 10—that we hereby invite all our people to join us in memorialising the General Conference; setting forth to that body, that an unscrupulous party has, by misrepresentation and deception, obtained the control of our conference, and is using its power ostensibly to sustain law and order, but really to "crush out" vital piety among us; adopting measures and decissions that tend to destroy true christian liberty, which has been the boast of Methodism; investing some of the more prominent *means* of the party with the dignity of judicial decisions as a pretext for *crushing* out, and driving from the church all,—people and ministers, who can not yield to its sway.—And we hereby invoke the General Conference to restore to the church and to our conference the six expelled ministers who are the victims of injustice and oppression.

Resolved 11—That the following named brethren:—Isaac M. Chesbrough, Russell Wilcox, and John Cannon be a committee to prepare a memorial to General Conference for the signature of our people on their respective charges.

AN APPEAL.

TO THE MEMBERS OF THE M. E. CHURCH, AND ALL PERSONS WHO RESPECT THE RIGHTS OF HUMANITY AND RELIGION.

Dear Brethren:—Allow me to present to you a candid statement of the facts in reference to my expulsion from the M. E. Church.

The Journal of the Genesee Conference for Oct. 13th, 1859, contains the following record:

Resolved, That John A. Wells be expelled from the Genesee Conference, and from the M. E. Church.

The charges which furnished the occasion for the above action, are as follows:

I hereby charge Rev. J. A. Wells with,

1st, *Contumacy*—in recognising as a minister, by admitting to his pulpit, and holding religious meetings in connection with B. T. Roberts, an expelled member from this Conference.

2d, *Disobedience to the order of the Church*, in going into the bounds of other brethren's charges, and holding religious meetings. (Signed) E. M. Hopkins. (Dated) Brockport, Oct. 1st, 1859.

It would be tame, indeed, for me to say that I am dissatisfied with the above action of the Conference. A blow has been struck at the vitals of christian liberty. I do not feel that I am guilty of contumacy, or disobedience to the order of the church; neither, if I were guilty to the extent of the specifications, could I believe the severest penalty known in ecclesiastical discipline, ought to be inflicted on me. I now make my appeal to you, and hope to be received and treated in accordance with the verdict which your candor and religion shall render.

I admitted, on my trial, that I had permitted B. T. Roberts to speak in my pulpit; and that I had attended and took part in religious meetings conducted by him. Also, that I had preached, in a few instances, within the bounds of other brethren's charges. There was nothing material proved in addition to this.

I showed in my defense:—

1st, That B. T. Roberts, since his expulsion, had been admitted to the M. E. Church on trial, and licenced to exhort, and as such I had received him. Bishop Simpson had decided that an error or illegality on the part of an administrator of discipline, does not invalidate the title to membership of a person received into the church. So that Bro. Roberts was legally and properly a member of the M. E. Church on trial. Whether his license to exhort, given by Rev. C. D. Burlingham, he being recommended to do so by the unanimous vote of the society at Pekin, was valid, or not, according to the letter of the law, it was, at least, a good reason in favor of my allowing him to speak. I could not forbid a man to speak in my pulpit, who came with such recommendations. If there is contumacy in this, it must consist in a refusal of absolute subjection to the will of the Buffalo Regency, and not in resistance to the reasonable authority of the church.

I showed in my defense:—

2d, That not one of the preachers on whose charges I had preached, had ever, by word or by letter, intimated to me that they were displeased with my preaching within the bounds of their charges, and also, that my Presiding Elder had never admonished me not to do so. If I was expelled for that, it certainly was a crime that none of the men who claimed to be injured thought enough of to speak to me about, though months elapsed between its commission and the conference.

I contend that I am expelled from the church for no crime whatever; either against the word of God, or the Methodist discipline. In those things for which I was expelled, I have not violated my obligation to God, nor transcended my rights as a Methodist preacher.

1. I am not blamable in recieving Bro. Roberts as I did. I received him, and treated him as an exhorter. It was not proved that I had done more than this. His relation to the church, and the license which he held, fully entitled him, according to the discipline and the usage of Methodism, to all the respect which I paid him. But I had higher reasons than these for doing as I did. I had for many years regarded Bro. Roberts as a devoted servant of God, eminent for his usefulness. I really believed that his expulsion from the church was only the result of hatred, aroused by his faithful denunciations of sin, and that he was, in the sight of heaven, as much a servant of God, and a minister of the gospel, after his expulsion as before it. I could not do less than receive him. To have forbidden him to speak in my pulpit, would have been a sin against God that I would not bear in the judgment, for all worlds.

2. I have not sinned in preaching within the territories claimed by other preachers. Simply preaching the gospel is all that I did. I was not charged with doing more. So that the solution of the question, Has one preacher any right to preach on another's territory? will make me guilty or innocent. The commission which God gave me is, "Go into all the world." I was ordained an Elder in the church of God. Now, if there is any thing in our church order limiting my right to preach to one small charge, or cutting me off from any particular place, let it be shown. In joining the itinerant ranks of Methodism, we do so far surrender our right of choosing our field of labor, as to allow the President of the conference to appoint where we shall preach; but we do not so surrender our rights, that he or any power on earth, can appoint where we can not preach. To make such a surrender, would be treason against God.— The discipline provides penalties for the preacher who refuses to go to his work, but it is nowhere made a crime to preach the gospel off from his charge.

I have foreborne to speak of others who are my companions in the same tribulation, partly because I left the seat of the conference before the adjournment, and do not know how far the work of decapitation has proceeded; and, partly, because I prefer that they should speak for themselves. The charges against eight preachers were nearly the same as those on which I was condemned, viz: contumacy and disobedience to the order of the church. The conference, on the second day of its session, adopted a series of Resolutions which amount to an *ex post facto* law, according to which every preacher's character was to pass. Every preacher who was supposed, during the year past, to have violated the code contained in the Resolutions, had his character arrested. No man could pass till he had testified his penitence for having violated them, (before they existed,) and promised to observe them in the future.

To what extent this persecution will be carried, the future alone can reveal. The majority of the conference are evidently determined, by raising the mad-dog cry of Nazaritism, to drive out of the church all who have religion enough not to endorse their measures. What others may do I cannot tell; but, as for myself, I am yet firmly attached, in heart, to the M. E. Church. I believe her doctrines and love her discipline. I have appealed to the General conference. I shall get back into the church again, if I can.

J. A. WELLS.

www.ingramcontent.com/pod-product-compliance
Lightning Source LLC
Chambersburg PA
CBHW030011040426
42337CB00012BA/742